The Earth Manifesto

THE EARTH
MANIFESTO

*Saving Nature
with Engaged Ecology*

David Tracey

RMB

Rocky Mountain Books
www.rmbooks.com

Library and Archives Canada Cataloguing in Publication

Tracey, David, 1959-, author
    The earth manifesto : saving nature with engaged ecology / David Tracey.

(RMB manifesto series)
Includes bibliographical references.
Issued in print and electronic formats.
ISBN 978-1-927330-89-0 (bound).— ISBN 978-1-927330-90-6 (html).—
ISBN 978-1-927330-91-3 (pdf)

    1. Nature conservation—Citizen participation. 2. Human ecology.
I. Title. II. Series: RMB manifesto series

QH77.3.C57T73 2013   333.72   C2013-903119-7
C2013-903120-0

Printed in Canada

Rocky Mountain Books acknowledges the financial support for its publishing program from the Government of Canada through the Canada Book Fund (CBF) and the Canada Council for the Arts, and from the province of British Columbia through the British Columbia Arts Council and the Book Publishing Tax Credit.

 Canadian Heritage Patrimoine canadien

 Canada Council for the Arts Conseil des Arts du Canada

 BRITISH COLUMBIA ARTS COUNCIL
Supported by the Province of British Columbia

The interior pages of this book have been produced on 100% post-consumer recycled paper, processed chlorine free and printed with vegetable-based dyes.

 FSC MIX Paper from responsible sources FSC® C016245

Contents

Introduction

If you ever get the feeling you live in a critical time, you're not alone. Many of us sense big change in the air, and not necessarily for the better. History is about to turn on decisions we make or ignore, but the implications are so ominous we avoid them in daily conversation. That doesn't make the crisis go away. As environmental threats loom, our social angst rises like static before a storm. Alienation has grown to the level of an epidemic. Depression is expected to become the second leading cause of disability before the decade is over. One of the worst symptoms of living out of sync is feeling powerless, the awful notion that our problems are so big and so entrenched that we have no control over where we're going.

That last part isn't true. We do have numbers, and conviction, and power, much more than we've been led to believe. We just haven't put those together yet.

This book was written to help. As a manifesto for the Earth, it looks at our planet-sized problems and offers ground-level solutions. These start with the individual, the personal scale at which we interact with our surroundings and the place where we can practise groundtruthing, a way to reconnect with nature even in the cities where we live. The ultimate goal is to unite individuals into communities that will transform our relationship with the living Earth. The point of this book is to say we can survive the crisis by rediscovering an affinity for nature which will help us reclaim our right to thrive in it.

Too big? Too bold?

No. Not when our house is on fire and all the champions of a green planet are called to the rescue. We must save our home from the profiteers who would sell the birthright of their own children. We who stand on the side of life must declare our understanding of the crisis, and how we intend to fix it – make manifest that which is right.

The Earth Manifesto is an appeal to people who care. That means most of us, even if we've been led to believe we don't because we're too busy, or shouldn't because we're not the experts, or can't because the system is rotten and politicians are all bad and the ice caps are already melting and what difference can one person make anyway?

That's pessimism, and it has no place here. What good has it ever done? Yes, the rich have been gaming the system to get even richer as they threaten our collective future. Yes, the elections that should be an antidote can get derailed by the squabbles of corporate-backed candidates and their media enablers. It's no wonder a common response to political events today, even among youth, is apathy. But indifference won't douse the flames and acquiescence won't help us discover how much we can do, because both go against who we really are.

We have evolved as humans to be better than some small, timid response to emergencies. If someone were to run into the room and shout, "Omigod! A little girl is trapped in a well and the water's rising. Someone please help!" who among us wouldn't drop everything? Who would not race to the door and do anything it takes to save something so precious?

Hope is a strategy too. Most of us have it inside, and in full measure, but only when others around us are sharing the same goal do we muster the courage to let it out into the light. That time is now.

Note that we're not concerned here with the crisis deniers; they can be dismissed in a paragraph. Some people can never imagine a change that would interrupt their plunder. We know the world's scientists have spoken with near unanimity on global warming and the threat it presents, yet a few rich people with the help of their news conglomerates have invented a fake debate that has stalled crucial action for years. Let's ignore them. They're on the wrong side of history and they won't win. More interesting and more useful are the rest of us, the future.

The larger list of people who care includes those who are confused. It's understandable. Given the predicament, we should be wary of anyone touting pat explanations and easy solutions. We realize the complexity of the problems. We understand the world is on the brink of something. And we're willing to act to make a difference. But everything is moving so fast and the issues seem so convoluted that it's difficult to know just what to think. Our brains are obviously important – why else would companies spend billions of dollars every year in advertising just to get into them – but how can we be sure we're channeling our energy in the right direction?

A key lesson of this book is to look for answers in the living Earth.

We can begin by reconnecting with the nature surging through everything, including our own bodies. For this to happen we need a physical location, a site we can identify with and learn from through groundtruthing, a way of engaging with a place that matters.

In our frenetic urban lives we may have lost an intimate connection to the natural world, but we still have the capacity for it. The affinity for life is bred within us. It can be rediscovered. It takes patience to sit and listen to things you didn't know had a voice, but the answers are there, and once you connect, change begins. We need more people who can do this with the resolve to heal an ailing environment. Groundtruthing provides an opportunity for anyone to develop the wisdom they need to become "grounded."

Finding our rightful place in nature can happen anywhere, even in a crowded urban area. In fact, cities are precisely where it will have to happen, because that's where most of us in the world now live. The best cities are cosmopolitan mixes that encourage new ways of thinking. A combination of cultural diversity and social cohesion makes these places fertile ground for innovative approaches to our current predicament. Add the abundant supply of human energy driving an exciting city forward and you have the ingredients for a revolution.

Engaged Ecology, or E^2, is a method for finding one's place in the natural world and using it as a tool for Earth-conscious activism. It's not the only course available for addressing our environmental quandary, and it may not fit some people at all. But it's offered here, in solidarity with those resolved to help a degraded planet, as a suggestion, in particular to anyone who senses the importance of our time but has yet to act. This part is critical. Action is everything. When enough of us no longer consent to the death spiral of the status quo, and choose instead to engage with the forces of life, we can regain control. Those who love the Earth will defend it, and together we'll heal our only home.

You've just read the message of this book. The rest is details. But before you skip ahead, consider that Engaged Ecology doesn't work by skimming. Inspiration is a start and we need good intentions, but mostly we need people to be aware, and then to care, and then to take a stand. Committed people working together can do the heavy lifting it will take to help us win.

This book explains how that can happen in two parts. Part One has the theory in three chapters, each describing one of Three Big Ideas. Part Two is the practice. Its three chapters cover the Three Big Steps on what to do. Together these add up to the Six Laws of Engaged Ecology.

In Chapter One, Nature Is Here, we explore how everything is connected and how inter-dependence is the world's operating system. If nature is one, it follows that we're a part of it. In Chapter Two, Wilderness Is Within, we look into our affinity for natural places where wildness can still happen, including within our own minds. Chapter 3, Cities Are Alive, deals with the need to expand our relationship with the wilderness to support the Earth and us in the urban areas where we live.

How? Chapter 4, The Earth Is Our Witness, introduces groundtruthing as a way to engage with a place where nature is worth saving. This leads to Chapter 5, We Have the Right to Clean Air, Pure Water, Healthy Soil, which discusses the political work needed to save these places under siege. In Chapter 6, Engaged Ecology Creates a Community, we see how the campaign is shared, leading us back to interdependence and completing the circle.

Engaged Ecology joins thoughts and deeds in collective action to support our only environment. When shortened to E^2, for E-squared, it suggests that ecology and engagement feed each other, creating a self-generating combination. Like a seed, E^2 needs only to be planted and nurtured. Once it sprouts, it can grow on its own.

The Six Laws of Engaged Ecology
1. Nature Is Here
2. Wilderness Is Within
3. Cities Are Alive
4. The Earth Is Our Witness

PART ONE
Three Big Ideas

Nature Is Here

Good news. You, dear reader, citizen of the planet, eco-warrior for a better world, do not have to go looking for nature. You're already there.

You may live in a concrete high-rise on a busy street. You may keep warm with central heating and see by electric light and view the world mostly through a flat screen. But you are no less a child of the natural Earth than were our tree-dwelling ancestors. You are a part of the grand flow of all things and you have an important role to play in keeping it going.

Trouble is, you don't know it. Or maybe you know it but you don't feel it. Or you feel it but have yet to figure out how to act on it.

Engaged Ecology can help open that door, the one that leads outside. You don't have to be out under the sky to get the concept, but it will help later when you plot how to connect with the web of life that supports us. For now, we're interested in the idea. E^2 revolves around a simple but deep notion, universal enough to be taken for a law, that Nature Is Here, wherever you are.

You can always find the true north of this law by remembering interdependence. It means everything is connected. This is more than a charming sentiment. It's a fact, the way things work in our universe, the structural glue that holds everything together. Ignore this fact, or abuse it, and you may fail: witness industrial society built around the flawed idea that poisoning one part of our nest won't affect the rest.

Understanding interdependence is essential to get "ecology," the relatively new science of the relationships between living things and their environment. German scientist Ernst Haeckel coined the term in 1866 from the Greek *oikos* for "home" and *logia* for "study." It reached household popularity a century later when it was picked up by environmental activists campaigning against pollution. Yet our understanding of the interconnectedness of life is actually much older.

The concept was explained 2,500 years ago

through Buddhist philosophy which said the nature of reality is emptiness. This doesn't mean a void, but rather that all things are empty of independent existence. Entities are "real" only in the sense of their relationships to others. Conventional reality is still with us; the chair I'm sitting in is solid enough to hold me up. But ultimately the chair and the "me" in it are mental constructs. By mistaking them for autonomous and permanent objects, we end up grasping for a world of things which are actually a series of events, a flow in which everything is connected.

Not an easy concept to grab onto. If a visual helps, picture Indra's Net, a Buddhist metaphor describing a net over the deity Indra's palace that spreads out to infinity. Each knot of the net holds a jewel. In each jewel can be seen a reflection of all the other jewels. A dot painted on one jewel would instantly appear in the rest. Thus the part contains the whole and the whole has no part which is isolated or disconnected.

Still not an easy concept. Maybe science can help. Quantum physics is now confirming at the subatomic level what Buddha said centuries ago, that all things are interdependent. In quantum mechanics, objects are not isolated, determined things, but possibilities. Einstein himself had trouble seeing how one half of a particle could determine the properties of the other half even if they happen to be separated. He said it would require "spooky action at a distance." Yet quantum entanglement experiments conducted since his death have shown the great thinker was wrong on that point. Nevertheless, Einstein got the big picture right when he said:

A human being is a part of the whole, called by us the "Universe," a part limited in time and space. He experiences himself, his thoughts and feelings, as something separated from the rest — a kind of optical delusion of his consciousness. This delusion is a kind of prison for us, restricting us to our personal desires and to affection for a few persons nearest us. Our task must be to free ourselves from this prison by widening our circles of compassion to embrace all living creatures and the whole of nature in its beauty.

Who wouldn't agree? Certainly we could stand to widen our circles of compassion. And yes, we should embrace the nature on which we all depend, and learn to see it holistically. We need to realize it's more about systems than objects, processes over events, circles instead of lines. Great notion, it all adds up, and having someone like Einstein say so definitely helps. Three cheers for interdependence.

But then look at the world we've made and continue to make. The ideas we find inspiring and the lives we end up leading do not match. We may lament the gap and yearn for some deeper connection, something that will let us feel more alive, yet we don't do anything about it. Instead we hustle every day to further a system we know is broken. What the hell has happened to us?

Historians argue about when we lost it and cut our own ties to nature. Were our savannah-roaming ancestors that much more in touch with their natural surroundings? Surely they were, but who really knows whether the life of a "noble savage" was brutish or blissful. We don't accord people back then a level of individual variation depending on circumstance or personality the way we do for ourselves today, but maybe their ultimate experiences were not so different. Maybe they too lived out their days in a range of emotions that could shift a dozen times before breakfast.

Some deem the Bible a ripe target for directing its subjects to go forth and dominate nature. But Judeo-Christianity has no monopoly on ecological catastrophe. Civilizations have been known to collapse from as far back as archaeologists have managed to dig up their remnants, some 40 major ones so far according to Jules Pretty in *The Earth Only Endures*.

Jared Diamond explains in *Collapse: How Societies Choose to Fail or Succeed* that their wounds were often self-inflicted through the misuse of natural resources. It turns out even a robust society is a fragile thing which may not be able to withstand the clear-cutting of its trees or the depletion of its soil.

More recently, thanks to resilient pockets of indigenous knowledge that have survived the cultural tsunami of modernity, we still have the stories of those who felt themselves a part of nature rather than its master. Consider the expression used as a greeting or prayer by some

Native American cultures, which also happens to be a pithy summation of the whole idea of interdependence: "All my relations."

In our day, the materialism of science is sometimes blamed for being a mechanistic view of reality that objectifies nature. Western science – which, let's not forget, is great when you need a kidney transplant – has also given us a world view that hasn't been entirely good for the world. From the time of the scientific revolution in the seventeenth century, we've believed that truth is objective, value-free and best discovered by dissecting a thing into ever smaller parts until we can know precisely how it's put together. Nature in this picture is one more machine, also understood by being reduced to its parts. Rather than the traditional wisdom's concept of nature as pervasive, and as essential to life as our mother, in the materialist view the idea of a living Earth is a non-starter.

Put the mechanistic view of nature together with capitalism's unchecked appetite for profit and we can see why corporatism continues to rise even as we burn through billions of years worth of fossil fuels in just decades. If there is no living nature on which we all rely, it's easier to ignore or accept the damage being done to parts of it. Even more oddly, though we deny the notion of life to the Earth, there are courts which consider corporations to be alive to the point of sharing rights with humans. Thus we're led to something approaching worship for an economic system that gets fussed over daily like a recalcitrant child as we check it for signs of growth, decay, rejuvenation and other metaphors borrowed from nature.

Our shift in the last two centuries from farms to cities has widened the culture–nature split. For all their attractions, cities were also seen as necessary evils, their pollution-spewing factories and crowded living conditions contributing to pestilence and bad manners. The remedies were to be visits to the natural idyll of the countryside on weekend trips or, for those who couldn't get away, city parks which would replicate the healing properties of nature through fresh air and picturesque landscapes.

It's not that it was wrong to soften the hard edges of the city with greenery. The songbirds would agree with us that every patch helps. But by confining the opportunities to experience nature to the boundaries of parks, we legitimized the idea of nature as separate from ourselves.

A similar notion was behind the nineteenth-century drive to create national parks. Again, good thing we did this or some spectacular swaths of land would now be buried under strip malls. But national parks also treated nature as a thing to be measured and corralled, revered and preserved, in pieces. We ignored the part about how, if everything is connected, nature can't simply be taken as something on the other side of a fence. It has to be recognized as here too, even in our big cities.

Sometimes it takes an extreme event to remind us how nature is always here. Hurricane Katrina in 2005 was a lesson in reckless development on a flood plain. A lesser-known example happened in Vancouver a few years ago, though few people at the time connected the dots to ask why.

On December 15, 2006, a windstorm hit the west coast. That wasn't surprising, winter being the season for storms, but this one was harsher than most. In some places the gusts reached hurricane force. The soil was saturated already from heavy downpours in the weeks before that had gone on long enough to muddy the drinking water from landslides into reservoirs. During the night of December 15, the strong winds and soft ground were a combination punch. In Vancouver's iconic nature area downtown, Stanley Park, 10,000 trees were uprooted or snapped into pieces.

It may have been just another freak weather event, the kind we now seem to get every year, or it could have been a more alarming notice that the world was indeed shifting into something new. People talked about warmer ocean currents and altered weather patterns and how climate change must be happening here and now. There was some mention of increased greenhouse gases and the global scale of the problem, but not so much about how we may have been more directly responsible.

In 2006 professor Renyi Zhang at Texas A&M University was already putting together research that found pollution from Asian factories changing the weather across the Pacific. His study, funded by the National Science Foundation and NASA and published in the *Proceedings of the National Academy of Sciences* the following year, linked factory emissions from places such as China with more severe weather systems running through the Pacific storm track.

"The pollution transported from Asia makes storms stronger and deeper and more energetic," he said. "It is a direct link from large-scale storm systems to [human-produced] pollution."

We blame China for building still more coal-burning power plants that spew the pollutants that affect our weather and crush our forests, but where do they get the stuff? British Columbia mining companies have been doing a roaring business selling to Chinese industrialists. They helped turn that country into a net importer of coal in 2009. And just what are the Chinese doing with all that Canadian coal? Powering the factories that churn out the cheap stuff we line up to buy at Walmart.

University of Washington atmospheric chemist Dan Jaffe has also studied emissions from Chinese factories. He suspected they were riding the jetstream across the Pacific, so he drove five hours northwest of Seattle to the tip of the country to look for them. The rainforest area at Cheeka

Peak is said to have some of the cleanest air in the United States, as prevailing winds prevent any contamination from the rest of the continent. Even in a pristine, undeveloped, "natural" area like Cheeka Peak, Jaffe found mercury, sulfates and ozone dropping out of the air from Asia.

"There is no place called away," Jaffe told *Discover Magazine*'s David Kirby. "We need to be concerned. There is no Planet B. We all live downwind."

Interdependence is the Earth's source code. It's the explanation for how things work.

It can also be considered a tool. We use interdependence through its expression in biodiversity, which is a way to describe the web of all life on which we depend for survival. If you ever have a difficult choice to make on an environmental intervention, it can help to gauge the results. If one choice adds more biodiversity by increasing the number of species of plants, animals, insects, birds etc., choose it. Avoid choices that would decrease biodiversity, with the extreme example in that case being a monoculture.

We know from ecology that a monoculture,

although useful on an industrial farm where a single crop can be harvested mechanically, is actually weak. One pathogen or a single weather event may ruin the whole operation. Monocrops are not naturally found in the wild, which could be why we tend to find the sameness unsettling or boring in a landscape, though that point has yet to reach the planners and architects and bureaucrats who design our cities.

It isn't always an easy choice. The world is more complex than that, and we can't count on the convenience of clearly good vs. clearly evil decisions. In 1999 when the Makah tribe on the west coast of Washington said they would resume a custom that had been outlawed for 70 years by killing a grey whale, many environmentalists were scandalized. Animal lovers were the most outspoken against the plan, while First Nations supporters were more likely to favour it.

How could biodiversity have helped sort through a dilemma like that? On a species level, the single animal the Makah whalers ended up taking did not greatly diminish the whale recovery effort. Little harm was done, although to be fair we don't know what goes through the minds of cetaceans when one of their community is attacked.

We know more about the impact the hunt had on the whalers and their families on shore. Months of hard training went into restoring the tradition, and the intense public scrutiny had a big impact on the tribe's desire to reset its own cultural foundations. Still not an easy decision, but it should be considered that biodiversity includes us and our culture. It's also worth considering that not all ecological thinkers would accept this idea of humans claiming a place at the biodiversity table, knowing our history of hogging everything on it.

We have treated nature with contempt for so long it's surprising we still have such a romantic notion of it. We call a collection of trees that hasn't been logged a virgin forest, a strange form of compliment. It reinforces our idea of real nature as something pure and unsullied. We also at various times see nature as a teacher, nature as our progenitor, nature as a redeemer. There's the benevolent nature of fawns and daisies, also the violent nature of bears and tornadoes.

Sometimes we hear that nature is always right

and the problems we now have with it are a just punishment for our transgressions. A related opinion agrees that the environment is in trouble because of stupid humans and so, good riddance, the world will be better off without us, let the rats and cockroaches rule.

There are elements of truth in these ideas, but also muddled thinking that doesn't help. That nature doesn't care about us makes sense. It doesn't choose favourites that way. In fact it doesn't really choose at all.

Even the most "natural" areas we appreciate today, such as remote wilderness sites, are the result of countless complex interactions among myriad species with any number of possibilities present in the early stages of development that could have changed things dramatically.

Watch what happens in your own neighbourhood to a city lot that gets cleared when a building is torn down. We know from experience which pioneer species of plants in a given area are likely to start colonizing that space, but not with certainty. The result may end up strikingly different from a similar lot just a block away, perhaps because a gust blew a particular airborne seed to one area but not the other. One hungry vole could devour the tender shoots of all the tree seedlings on a site, delaying or negating the expected forest. A random event can result in a completely different plant community hundreds of years later. The chaos theory works not just on butterflies in Malaysia but on our own street as well.

One thing we do know is that nature is dynamic. It is always changing. Even a climax-stage forest, where one kind of tree may tower over the rest for centuries, is teeming with organisms of many kinds, all growing, dying and being recycled back into the mix, and thus always in flux. Any particular time we happen to visit still offers no more than a snapshot in a place's natural history.

Because nature includes us, it invites the prospect of our working with it. Yes, this is manipulation, and yes, we often botch the job. That doesn't mean we can't or shouldn't try. Particularly in the cities, where we shouldn't leave to random events the possibility of sites not turning out to be the best for us and for the planet.

Rather it means we should act wisely, and respectfully, with humility and the realization that all things are connected and biodiversity makes a good measuring stick. Accepting a new role for people in their own environment is entirely within the realm of reinterpreting our romantic idea to agree that nature knows best, for we are part of it.

Not long before he died, Buddha sat before a crowd of followers at Vulture Peak to begin a teaching. But he didn't speak as usual. Instead he held up a flower. One of the more learned monks named Mahakashyapa smiled. Buddha recognized the achievement and chose Mahakashyapa as his successor to pass on the teachings. The whole is contained in the part, and a flower can be a microcosm for a world of truth.

Wilderness Is Within

Last chapter we used interdependence to say Nature Is Here, meaning wherever we are. But it gets even more intimate than that. Nature is also in our bodies and minds, two places where wilderness still reigns.

We know the idea of nature is a wide tent that can cover a lot of territory. One way to define it is to say nature is all things non-human. Animals and shrubs, bugs and fungi all fit in there. So would everything else under the sun apart from people and our creations, which fall under the category of culture. But we've seen already how this is a problem, because if nature is whole, how could we be excluded?

Nature in terms of location can be described as anywhere not developed, where the wilderness still exists. If the wilderness is defined as a place hosting the wild, this presents an opportunity where we might come in to bridge the nature–culture divide.

We love the wilderness. At least we love the idea of the wilderness. Where else would we go for religious epiphanies? Jesus in the desert. Aboriginal youth going walkabout in the outback. Tibetans circling the sacred Mt. Kailash. The list could go on, around the planet, and take in all kinds of spiritual beliefs and land forms.

Our reverence for outdoor experiences works just as well without a formal religious foundation. Ask a surfer about the mystical interface of water, wind and shore. Try anyone who's been lucky enough to have stood in some sublime wild area and felt the inclination to transcendence.

Wilderness has the allure of the siren song. We are drawn to its irresistible charm, a beauty so magnificent it can be transformative. In the wilderness we might explore what it means to be truly human, no longer bound by the artificial restraints of an indifferent or corrupt society.

We also invest in it our hopes for planetary salvation. Even if dwindling in number and size, wilderness areas are seen as our last refuge on Earth. These are the flickering candles we must protect so we can one day use them to light the torches that will illuminate our way back to a saner form of civilization.

But siren songs, of course, lead to peril, which is why the metaphor might still be useful here. Much as we believe we revere the wilderness, we also know it as raw, untamed and even dangerous. We're afraid of it.

The modern concept of wilderness in North America was borne in the minds of settlers from Europe. They had no problem recognizing the division between nature and culture. It was right there in front of the fort wall or cabin door. Wilderness was something that had to be overcome if you hoped to survive. Harsh weather, wild animals, angry natives whose land you took – all were things to be avoided.

Like the transition 10,000 years earlier when we shifted from hunting and gathering to agriculture, settling a wilderness area would first mean clearing the forest so the open soil could be planted. To protect the crops and the people tending them, a perimeter security fence would be erected. This would mark the line between inside, where life was ordered and under control, and outside, where the wild still happened with its potential chaos and menace.

Of course, this perception ran counter to generations of traditional thinking in which humans saw themselves less as nature's masters than its collaborators, if they thought in those terms at all. In indigenous cultures, we are told, people had conversations with the animals, the plants, even the places themselves, which they relied upon in order to live.

Some sites, deemed sacred, had to be asked permission before one would even think to enter. Food that was hunted or foraged would be offered gratitude for providing life with its death, a gesture of respect and also a reminder of the natural cycles which would one day include the eater. A mind that will think to ask forgiveness from a tree before cutting it down is already living in a different world, no matter the time or place, from one which looks at a forest and sees board feet.

We might still have these conversations with nature that allow us to be with the wild, but how would we start if we don't recognize it? You can't talk to something that isn't there. This isn't a malicious thing, our ignoring the possibility of a living Earth. We just don't care, certainly not enough to invest the potential other with a presence that would merit respect. Any of us today caught talking to a meadow or thanking a tree for its apples would probably be embarrassed. And yet we're not ashamed at having severed a connection to the natural world that once taught us who we were and where we stood.

This doesn't mean we don't feel the absence of this lost connection, or that it's gone for good. Children still have an easy gift for immersing into the spirit world of natural places and things. They can recognize or conceive lives we can't even see, at least they can until they get old enough to understand that our society considers it silly.

At some level many of us know we've lost something valuable in our stand apart from the wilderness. We may not be able to see the path to take us back, but that's no cause for giving up. We have the map still inside us. The wild still whispers through our bones. It guides us in curious ways.

Why else would we feel almost hypnotically at home in certain situations and places, such as when staring into a campfire, or absorbed in a walking rhythm, or sharing something important with our tribe – all vestiges of our ancestral past. Today we plant our yards in miniature versions of the savannah. We obsess over gardens that offer a glimpse into the miracle of life through plants that eat sunshine. We bring beasts, otherwise known as pets, inside to share our homes. We find nothing so fascinating as the company of other humans, and suffer greatly from its loss. In prison the worst punishment is solitary confinement.

The wilderness that is home to wild places is part of our DNA. We could never completely let go of the wild, even if we wanted to. To deny it is to deny ourselves, which we've tried, through industrial civilization, but it hasn't worked out. To rediscover our place in nature, one that can be found even in an urban world, we come to the second law of Engaged Ecology: Wilderness Is Within.

Some will argue we can't be wild, by definition, because as humans we're obviously the opposite, the antithesis of the animal world. We have speech and concepts and civilization. Ever since our species, *Homo sapiens*, won out over the Neanderthals, we've been the ones in control. We're at the top of the food chain, standing over the rest of an animal kingdom that doesn't even know there is an order to these things. We shape the world, not the other way around, even if mistakes made in our rise to dominance now seem world-sized.

But to look at it another way, are we really in control? Does the order we think we bring to the random world of nature extend as far as we believe if we can't even control ourselves? Have we not been fooling ourselves with a facade of orderly civilization as the opposite of chaotic nature?

Consider the ecosystems of our bodies, now assailed by inputs we never had to face during millions of years of evolution. How many new chemical concoctions are in our homes and on our plates that have never been tested on people? And why is cancer rising despite the billions of dollars we pour into defeating it? Every ecosystem has a limited capacity to cope with stress, and our bodies are no different. If we were truly in control, you would think we wouldn't be so thick as to heap toxins on our own plates. Even those animals we consider dumb are not stupid enough to eat things that add up to poison.

For more examples of how we're wild, look at your fingers, matched with opposable thumbs and perfectly sized to grab onto a branch to stop a fall. Even a newborn will grasp your twig-shaped finger with a surprisingly firm grip. Think of the strongest muscles you have, your legs, great for walking long stretches through a forest or across open grassland. Consider our eyes, good for spotting danger or food at a safe distance. Our bodies are wild too in the way a surprise makes our breath quicken into a gasp, sucking in oxygen which our suddenly rapid pulse races to the rest of the network.

Paul Shepard in *Coming Home to the Pleistocene* takes up the argument over whether humans are "domesticated." He concludes we're still genetically wild but tame. Like any captured animal, we're conditioned to appropriate behaviour in a household. But that doesn't mean we thrive there. We can be civilized, but never domesticated. Shepard concluded that modern living hid our inherent need for "diverse, wild, natural communities." This deprivation is so severe we end up with a litany of stress-related problems. But Shepard didn't expect to find the answer in the self-help section of the bookstore.

> Modern psychology, including "eco-psychology" and "environmental psychology," tends to portray the self in terms of individual choices about beliefs, possessions and affiliations rather than defining the self in terms of harmonious relations to others – including other species – and in terms of the ecological health of the planet.

For Shepard there was a distinction between wildness, meaning the living world with its habitats and species including us, and wilderness, which he thought was a concept invented by urbanized people needing an escape from their regimented and boring lives. He believed wildness was being destroyed by those out to turn wilderness into a tourist attraction.

But we all immerse into nature-based experiences of our own design according to our own circumstances, and the wilderness remains a powerful notion that still resonates even if it has the taint of human intervention. In Japanese gardening, heavily influenced by Zen, it's fine to show a visible manipulation of the environment to achieve a depiction of nature.

This seems a paradox but it's not seen as a problem, because Zen monk designers understood that a garden exists in two places: at the site itself and in the mind of the viewer. This understanding, centuries old, continues to inform Japanese ideas of nature. Importantly for us today, it suggests a way we might use the idea of wilderness to our benefit in developed cities.

Gary Snyder also discusses the wilderness in our minds. He says the "wild mind" is self-disciplined and self-managed, as is the wilderness, a place where "nobody has to do the management plan." He writes in *The Practice of the Wild*:

> The conscious agenda-planning ego occupies a very tiny territory, a little cubicle somewhere near the gate, keeping track of some of what goes in and out (and sometimes making expansionistic plots), and the rest takes care of itself. The body is, so to speak, in the mind. They are both wild.

What to do with this? We need to figure out how to live better with the wilderness within, using our own wild nature to advantage. For this we need places where it can happen, sites where outside nature and our own inner nature can coexist.

It is no small step to see the whole of nature and grasp the unity of life, but for some, visiting an unspoiled wilderness area is an opportunity to have it happen spontaneously. Yet even those sites may be less pure than we had thought, as with Cheeka Peak and its toxic fallout.

The planet is too small and we're too smart to believe we can continue to run or hide. We've lost our innocence when it comes to what the wilderness is all about. The sites we choose now to make our stand can't be restricted to outdated notions of nature as precious sanctuaries in far-off areas. Our task is to express ourselves as humans at home in nature in cities too.

Accomplishing this must begin with a skilful selection of places we decide to preserve or improve, using our best practices of biodiversity enhancement. But we probably needn't spend too much energy worrying about choosing the wrong place. Nature, the wild and wilderness can ultimately be found wherever we look, by definition, because we're there as part of it. And improving any site will only add to the greater good.

The idea is to expand the number and quality of places where we can experience nature to feel a part of all things, where our spirits can soar. When we come to love these places, we'll fight for them, and in that struggle protect key areas not only for our own enjoyment but for the web of life. For that we need to develop a new relationship with the wilderness.

It's time to grow out of our latent fear of wilderness as the foreboding places we're afraid to go, in the recesses of our minds, not just at physical sites.

We can start by admitting that the wilderness within is indeed scary and that delving into it involves risk. Few are comfortable with the sense of utterly letting go. Opening up means accepting the possibility of revealing parts of ourselves that are uncontrollable or ugly. There is also the potential that we will fail.

Similarly, on the physical level, saving or establishing wild areas in cities is a risk that some, starting with city bureaucrats and lawyers, are unwilling to consider.

Watch what happens when a resident suggests letting wilder edges grow around a local park, or tries to stop the limbing up of its trees to achieve the "eyes on the street" that lets everyone see through the site free of any dark or shady places. Fears bubble to the surface and break.

The manicured version of the English countryside is easy to understand as a park amenity, and serves its purpose, but we also need areas where dead trees are left to rot and brambles grow overhead, even if they are scary. Maybe even because they're scary. One of the problems of our litigious times is the lack of natural places for children at play to confront and overcome their own fears. Even if we could regulate the wilderness away, we would still need to find ways to brave that walk through the woods past the big bad wolf. It's an important part of growing up.

We should think not only of the risk in letting wilderness happen but also of the reward. Wilderness as home to the wild is about more than something uncontrollable – though that can be one of its charms. It's also about being free. Our psyches are called to the untamed and limitless. We need places that let us fulfill the urge to explore the wild and free nature of our own minds.

Today we're in the exciting early stages of building a new urban world. The cities we re-design to help us survive the present crisis and beyond will have to have places where wilderness thrives. Progress on this front must involve not only the part, although every pocket park and eco-habitat will help, but more importantly the whole as we realize the importance of fostering a wilderness that pervades all.

We know everything is connected. We should treat our wilderness within in this same spirit of interdependence. We should see it holistically, as if mind, body and spirit, and the balance between them, were all important to our health.

Just as we can learn to live and grow with wilderness on the outside that enhances biodiversity, we can learn to make better use of the wilderness within, which is our minds, so that both are allowed to prosper.

It sounds difficult and maybe it is, but it's also necessary, because to save important places means also to save ourselves. Only when we rediscover our natural affinity for the wild can we hope to reach our potential as citizens of the planet and be truly comfortable in our natural home.

Cities Are Alive

If cities can live, they can die too. Ubar, Vilcabamba and Machu Picchu. Angkor and Mandu, Paquimé and Cahokia, Humberstone and Wittenoom. All were born, grew, thrived, fostered drama in thousands of human stories and then disappeared.

Cities do not have an impressive record when it comes to longevity or, to use a current term, sustainability. Civilization is a history of cities lost and reclaimed by jungle plants or desert sands.

Sometimes we have just the memories or myths and not even the ruins. Where remnants can be studied, the collapse is often attributed to ecological blunder or economic decline, which can add up to the same thing. Lessons from these failed social experiments would probably be more disturbing if we were inclined to believe the plodding ancients had anything to teach us modern sophisticates about how to live together in large numbers.

The cities we know today will surely be ridiculed by future generations. Even in our time they're ripe targets for criticism. There seems to be something not to like for everyone.

We choose them to live in, by the billions, yet for many of us our relationship may be on a love–hate basis. We're all for the money and cultural diversity and vibrant human energy. Not so much the traffic and pollution and crime.

City life is not for everybody, nor should it try to be. Some people are just better suited to slower and quieter environs.

Small cities and towns, or rural districts, are a good choice for those too distracted by frenetic urban areas. But even these people might see the advantage in helping us build a future of healthy cities. Every urban area that succeeds means less pressure on the surrounding region from people in need of escape.

As it is, so few of our cities succeed. If people feel pressed in a place where they have a soul-killing job, an unhealthy home and dreary surroundings, what should we expect but dissatisfaction? At some point the frustration turns into detachment, and that can feed a negative spiral that makes city living worse in turn. This is happening now to enough people in enough places that it almost seems normal. Our urban areas seem to get more crowded and lonelier at the same time.

And even if they were friendly zones of endless bliss, we know our cities can't last the way we've built them up. They're the reason the Earth is sliding closer to a climate that would be disastrous for large swaths of people. Urban areas use up most of our resources and produce most of our waste.

So if cities are not meeting our needs and are leading us to catastrophe besides ... what are we thinking? Other than developers capitalizing on the cancer-like growth we've been told to call progress, who benefits from the way things are?

The future of cities must be designed on a new way of living we've never tried before. To succeed it will have to solve the conundrum of how to get millions of people in close proximity living meaningful lives in ways that do not suck the resources out of a small planet. This will require making cities we love because they let us know we're at home, in places where we can feel a part of all things living.

We could start by recognizing that Cities Are Alive. Not necessarily in the sense of being animate, with a measurable pulse, but rather like the Gaia hypothesis in which the Earth's physical and biological processes exist as a mutually supportive, self-regulating system.

Cities should be seen as complex, diverse, fascinating, dynamic places where nature and wilderness can flourish. From the wilderness in our undomesticated minds to the hardy flowers that eke out a bloom through gaps in the pavement, signs of life in cities abound. It's up to us to discover them, and where we can't, to introduce them.

Despite what we're conditioned to see, cities are natural places. Even the busiest block in a built environment is part of the organic Earth. The soil may be covered with concrete and the air polluted with new chemical compounds, but the potential for greenery is still there and would return in exuberance if we were to leave. Look at the abandoned blocks in Detroit where wild vegetation is already reclaiming the lawns and marching up the porches of sagging homes, the prairie coming back with exuberance.

Or observe an empty lot in your own city if it's left alone. Windblown or bird-dropped seeds will find any open patch of decent soil by the next growing season. The earliest colonizing trees start the arms race to capture sunlight, but the tactic to get their solar collector leaves open above the rest may cost them in stability. The fastest trees have the weakest branches, leaving them vulnerable to damage, and they have shorter lifespans as well. They can be taken as a temporary stage before the more mature trees of a climax forest get established. But even that will be temporary, for nature is a moving pageant that always has forces on the march that we would recognize if we took the time to look.

It may be tempting to think of the greener grass over the fence of some other city or neighbourhood as better than ours and more conducive to nature, but any downtown or inner city district is full of life and nature worth exploring.

The first place most people would look to find urban nature is probably their nearest park or garden. Both fit the bill, with life teeming from the tree canopy down to the shrubs to the perennial or annual plants and then the soil with its billions of organisms in every handful. But you don't have to limit your search for nature to areas already designated as green. There may be more going on, in terms of biodiversity and life, in less obvious places such as industrial zones, alleys, rooftops, canals, ditches, back yards, schoolyards, empty lots and more.

Even a narrow balcony on the 23rd floor of a high-rise building is an ecosystem in waiting, with just a few planted containers required to provide habitat for countless living things, from microbes to plants to butterflies and birds. Planted or not, that balcony space is still a part of the cycles of nature. Every rainfall on it is a reminder of hydrology in motion and a view of the weather systems sweeping through a region. If it permits a glimpse of the night sky, there's an opportunity to consider our place in the cosmos as clever apes on a tiny blue ball in a vast universe.

Cities are habitats for more creatures than we might expect. Some wild things have figured out how to prosper in urban areas and may already fit them better than we do. Like us, these edge species tend to be opportunistic, crafty types who soon work out how to flourish in the border areas between ecosystems. They can dine from a variety of sources and may find places to sleep by thinking beyond the obvious to look under sheds and up trees and on top of buildings. Raccoons and crows and skunks and coyotes all fall into this category. Joining them only recently have been bald eagles.

Some of our urban neighbours survive specifically because they do well among humans. The ginkgo tree is known as a living fossil which looks much the same today as it did millions of years ago. For a long time it was believed to have gone extinct in the wild. But because it was cultivated, we still have ginkgo trees today and their popularity has spread from small pockets of Asia to places around the world.

Ginkgo trees are also known as survivors, beautiful but tough specimens that can endure harsh urban stresses such as pollution. A ginkgo tree in Hiroshima just 1.1 kilometres from the epicentre of the atomic bomb stood through the force of the explosion and the subsequent radiation and remains today as a symbol of resilience.

Or consider the dandelion growing out of a crack in the urban pavement. We know this weed as a scourge that ruins the disposition of homeowners with its temerity to interrupt a perfect green lawn with impertinent blasts of yellow. And what happens if we don't soon yank the interloper out? The flower transforms into a globe of seeds, each equipped with its own tiny parachute, awaiting merely a puff to launch into the airstream and drop into new territory to expand the assault.

We know hundreds of corporate logos but very few plants, and dandelions are one of the rare perennials most of us recognize. They make our short list because of their notoriety, which says something about the control of our opinions on good and bad nature. It's not an easy job convincing people to soak their own ground with poisons that cancer specialists insist should be illegal. But the American lawn care industry is said to be worth $40-billion a year, so people continue to be outraged at the sight of a flower and the toxic rivers still flow.

Can we learn to appreciate a more generous notion of urban nature? Consider that a dandelion will open its flower in the morning to greet the sun and close it in the evening to sleep. It can represent three celestial bodies, the sun in flower, the moon as a puff ball and stars when the seeds take flight.

Some 93 species of insects have been recorded visiting dandelion flowers for pollen. Dandelions bloom for a longer period than almost any plant in our gardens, making them an important food source for bees in the early and late season when other stores are scarce.

In Victorian times young dandelion leaves were gathered for the tables of the wealthy. They're just now making their way back into local stores as a gourmet item. The leaves taste sweet in a salad or stir-fry if picked before they get too big, or you can cover the young plants for up to two weeks to blanch them, producing a pale-coloured leaf without the chlorophyll that produces bitterness. The flowers are edible too, and can serve as salad decorations or be made into dandelion wine. Even the roots can be roasted to make a hot beverage substitute for coffee.

Herbalists know dandelion as a diuretic, appetite stimulant, aid to digestion, immunity-booster and more. The botanical name, *Taraxacum officinale*, comes from the Greek *taraxos* for disorder and *akos* for remedy, put together with the Latin *officinalis* for "of pharmaceutical value."

If a hated "weed" can be appreciated as an example of nature in cities, how about a common bird? Like the dandelion, the pigeon is a species introduced to North America which found conditions favourable enough to "naturalize."

Pigeons mate for life but are known for being gregarious, meaning they hang out in flocks, although in this case some think it more appropriate to use the word "gangs."

Pigeon flocks range in size from about a dozen to hundreds of birds, depending on the food available at the time. One of the advantages of gang life is shared intelligence. Pigeons learn, or least mimic, useful behaviour from each other. One flock in Sweden became known for its daily ride on the Stockholm subway, walking from the platform into a car to travel to a shopping centre that had plenty of cafés and food sources.

Japanese scientists discovered that pigeons can

be trained to recognize the difference between paintings by Picasso and Monet (the birds were given a food reward for pecking a lever when shown one or the other). The results held up even when new examples of the artists' works were shown. A related experiment demonstrated that pigeons were comparable to humans, or at least college students, in their ability to distinguish between Cubism and Impressionism.

There are also advantages to gang life in shared security: one bird can warn the rest when to take off. Curiously, pigeons seem to prefer areas downtown crowded with us. Also oddly, even in busy pedestrian areas they're typically seen on the pavement in easy grabbing range while the branches of nearby trees are empty. Evidently they're smart enough to know we've changed our preferences from the days when pigeons were considered tasty, a role since assumed by the chicken.

Even their group behaviour shows signs of clever thinking. Luc-Alain Giraldeau and researchers in Montreal found individual pigeons there freely choosing among flocks throughout the day based on resources. A bird could spend the morning with one group, the afternoon with another and join a third in the evening. They go wherever the action is in terms of getting what they want. A pigeon watching our group behaviour might come to a similar observation about us.

If we can learn to admire these "rats with wings," maybe we can rediscover an appreciation for the wild in the city in all kinds of forms. Nature doesn't stop at municipal borders, and every urban neighbourhood has rich worlds of life to explore. Developing a sense for the communities of other species sharing our space might be the introduction we need to explore a healthier relationship with our urban environment.

The city is a cooperative. We forget this in our limited view, distracted by property and how it gets carved into public or private spaces. But really, cities are mass collections of mutually supportive people who pretty much get along.

Cities are the future and will be for generations to come. In 1800 some 3 per cent of the world's population lived in urban areas. Now more than half of it does and a million more people crowd into cities every week. We're now an urban species and unlikely to ever go back.

We even have a new term to describe the growing enormity of urban gatherings. When more than 10 million live together, they form a megacity. By 2015 there will be 22 megacities, some of which you may not even know. Chongqing? It's in southwest China. It has 32 million people.

China itself will add 350 million people to cities in the next 10 years. That's the equivalent of the entire population of the US See why it's crucial to get cities right?

At this news some will be certain they see the problem: too many people. But our biggest threat is not overpopulation, despite the common argument that says the world can't possibly support 7 billion or 9 billion or 15 billion people, so only when we get back down to a billion or so will we be secure. But cities have been collapsing for millennia, including back in the day when the world population was less than 200 million. The point is not how many, but how people live together.

Tokyo is now the world's biggest city, in terms of people sprawled in one urban expanse. It has 35 million. And it's livable. It hasn't made great environmental choices in many ways, and it draws on more resources than it should, and the vast numbers of people certainly make it feel crowded, but all those residents add up to a strength, too. Trains run everywhere because they're guaranteed a sizable ridership, so a private automobile isn't needed. Even the compact cars and trucks you do see in Tokyo reflect the innovation inspired by living with limited space. Like the transistor radio, small cars were a Japanese urban idea that swept the world.

When it comes to determining whether a city will prosper or decline, land matters. Decisions on land use define our quality of life today as well as our prospects for the future.

For example, some parts of nearly every city are reserved for nature, usually in the form of city parks. In North America we have accepted for over a century the idea that toddlers deserve precious space out of our limited real estate, so we turn sections of city parks over to playgrounds with swings and slides.

Some day we may decide it's also worth supporting the food future of those kids, along with the rest of their families, through areas set aside as agricultural zones for community gardens and production farms. We might also decide that children of all ages need wild areas to nurture our own relationships to nature that keep us sane and alive.

Land use decisions are typically made at City Hall, usually by politicians acting all too often under the influence of the citizens with the most money: developers. But not inevitably. Politics is a team sport. If you don't have the numbers, because of apathy or lack of awareness or a weak argument, you shouldn't be surprised when decisions go the other way and our cities end up looking as if they were designed by bloodless bureaucrats.

More important than the gridlines and structures of the official zoning areas are what Shakespeare said a city really was: its people. The character of a city is determined not by the politicians or planners or experts but by those who live, work and play in it every day. We create the culture.

This is why citizens need to get more deeply involved in how their cities are evolving. The battles are no longer merely about housing developments or traffic patterns, but the Earth itself. We can influence this best by caring for city places, creating spaces where wilderness can exist and we can engage with it.

There are countless ways this can be done, and often more creatively than anything you'll hear from a city staff report. As environmental artist Oliver Kellhammer says, "The city is a hackable space."

By taking on places and determining to make them better, we move from being spectators to participants. Once we actively involve ourselves in the look, shape and feel of a city, we begin to reclaim our rightful place as a part of it connected to the Earth.

The deepest way to establish a connection to your city is to dig into it. People love a place they plant themselves.

This works on the single level of, say, a neighbourhood tree-planting project to start a mini-orchard. It holds true for the bigger city beyond, and as we scale up it holds for the Earth too. If we can learn to see cities as living homes for nature, we can begin to treat them with care and respect and love.

We might consider ourselves fortunate to live in cities even as we grumble about their shortcomings. If cities are where the problems are, it means the solutions are here too. This puts us at the front edge of the battle. It means big responsibilities, but nothing we can't handle together.

Whether you start with a place that's small or large, pristine or fouled, each person who decides to care for a piece of urban land adds strength to a growing movement. As each place defended is joined to others, they create a network of meaningful sites that can eventually cover the Earth.

PART TWO
Three Big Steps

The Earth Is Our Witness

Raising awareness is important, but useless on its own. What good is ecological literacy without action? It would be like learning to read and then never picking up a book.

Engaged Ecology has two parts. Both are necessary for a connection.

We discussed ecology in Part One when we looked at nature and wilderness and the need to find them wherever we are. Part Two is about deepening our relationship with them through engagement. We are not just passively admiring nature, we are actively involved in planting it, maintaining it, improving it, defending it.

"Engaged" is used here in the sense of becoming a participant, as in the expression *engagé* to describe someone passionately committed to a cause.

Engagé comes from the old French for pledge. That speaks to the level of commitment we'll need if we hope to change the world. This can be a lifelong and life-changing dedication. You could also call it a devotion.

Engaged Ecology moves us from discovering an affinity for a place to becoming a part of it. In practice this can happen at various scales and levels of intensity, but E^2 is not so well suited to casual acceptance or vague approval. If it's going to work, you have to be into it.

Filipino novelist F. Sionil José is an example of someone who is *engagé*. In an interview with author Charlson Ong he noted the difficulty people have committing to a cause, and brought the idea back to a love for the land:

> One of the greatest tasks of Filipino writers really is how to make Filipinos remember. Not only to remember but to love this country. You don't have to teach farmers how to do that because they deal with the land, they love the land. It's the urbanized, the rich, who don't have that kind of affection for the land. And without that kind of affection for the land itself, we will go nowhere. And that starts with memory. We cannot blame

> colonialism all the time, it's a dead horse.
> We must really look within ourselves for
> the kind of love that will transcend us as
> individuals.

To be *engagé* is to enter a reciprocal relationship. This engagement unites you with a vision of a better world that can be realized through a site you choose.

Your target may be big or small, near or far. It can be your own backyard. Or a corner of the local schoolyard. A busy intersection that's been terrorizing pedestrians for too long. A chain link fence that could be draped with planting bags and lettuce seeds. A park or even a parking lot. It could be a city-long river that's buried under concrete. Or the city itself, or the watershed that replenishes it.

Someone ambitious might say it's the whole world and work accordingly, although for most, to achieve the kind of conversation with nature discussed in Part One will require finding a physical patch of ground nearby. You want to select somewhere important, a place that needs you.

The next step is to groundtruth it, which is a way to describe discovering the essence of a site by being with it. "Groundtruth" is both a verb: "to truly understand a place you have to groundtruth it," and a noun: "that site looks bare on Google Earth but the groundtruth tells a different story."

In scientific terms it refers to the practice of checking satellite-derived data by visiting the area in question. Used this way, groundtruthing can be a measuring tool to record information such as the actual number of trees on a site.

When we use it, there's a qualitative aspect as well: not just the number of trees but the fact that when a certain part of a grove catches the late afternoon sun on a winter's day it can be delightful. Just as science can probably reproduce all the compounds that go into a fruit but will never match the experience of biting into a crisp apple under the tree from which it was just picked, groundtruthing reveals information on levels deeper than our vocabulary can describe.

Groundtruthing lets us avoid the mistakes or lies made possible by detachment. It's grand to live in a time when a thin box pulled out of a shirt pocket can zoom in to an aerial view of a site half-way around the globe. But every new technology comes with costs, such as the delusion that we can know a place at a distance.

You could study all the statistics and learn that China is surging, its economy is roaring, more people are shopping all the time. You could also learn that it has problems with pollution bad enough to be called an "airpocalyse." But only when you get to Beijing can you truly grasp what it's like on days when the air is hard to breathe.

Maybe one day someone will create an app that will make virtual nature seem so immersive we won't even miss the real thing. We can only hope not. For now, groundtruthing relies on too many organic inputs to be replicated by a machine.

In the environmental design profession, groundtruthing can be taken as a measure of respect, something we're more used to hearing from indigenous cultures. In a busy studio when competition is tight and trips away from the desk may not count as billable hours, the temptation is to just zap out an easy landscape plan on the computer. But this is bad form and prone to result in bad design, because until you sit with a place you can't honestly expect to know how to best shape it.

Groundtruthing is something we know already even if we haven't called it that. We've all had the experience of a sensual interaction with a place that let us get it. Think of nature-inspired moments where you felt what it means to be in touch with the elements: how the first glimpse of the ocean on a stifling day cooled you down, or the cackle of a raven watching a busy street seemed perfectly timed as a funny comment, or the smell of pine-scented air near the peak of a mountain provided just the boost you needed to go on.

To groundtruth a place is to engage with it using all senses available. Who feels it knows it. Jesse Wolf Hardin tells Derrick Jensen in *How Shall I Live My Life*:

> Your door to the entire world is located where your feeling body touches the giving ground. Your bare feet, your rear end, the few square inches of absolute contact are points of connectivity between yourself and millions of years of organic process. And

the way to fully experience that connection
is by disengaging our mental tape loops,
our voice tracks, the constant commentary
that keeps us perpetually anticipating the
future or criticizing our self about the past
rather than tasting the muffin we're eating
right now. Then we can experience the world
around us – as well as within us – like the
awakened, hungering, feeling, responding,
caring creature selves we really are.

Once you open yourself up to the flow of
nature through groundtruthing, it can speak to
you in ways you may not expect. Already some
will dismiss this as a woo-woo sentiment, but is
it really so difficult to believe a place can hold its
own energy, something we can sense but never
explain?

Few people would be comfortable buying or
renting a home based solely on pictures of it. We
know every place has its own vibe, something
that can't be measured but is definitely felt.

The spiritually attuned say holy sites where
advanced masters have lived or practised still
resonate with some of their power. Again, this

could be dismissed as crazy talk, but ask one of the millions of sports fans who would swear they feel something when entering the hallowed ground of a great stadium.

Even though we live in a materialist time, the notion that sites can have a spiritual presence has survived our march out of nature into modernity. People are most likely to experience this in the wilderness. But it can be found almost anywhere through groundtruthing, the act of being with a place that inspires Engaged Ecology.

When Buddha chose his place to achieve the final stage of enlightenment, he found a patch of ground under a ficus tree in northern India. He sat there in meditation for six days, going deeper to reach the profound realization that would later move millions. Just before getting to that level, according to Buddhist legend, he was tempted by Mara, a projection of his ego, asking by what right he thought he could understand everything.

Buddha responded by touching the ground to say the Earth was his witness. This gesture is reproduced everywhere today in Buddhist statues and iconography. It grounds the teaching in the land. All we have to work with is right here, wherever we are.

Food democracy activists may be interested to learn that in his other hand Buddha holds a begging bowl. Even at the peak moment of his long spiritual journey, the daily reality of food is still right at hand.

You don't have to be philosophical or spiritual to look for the "spirit of the place." This is also sometimes called the "genius of the place" after the Roman *genius loci*.

Poet Alexander Pope declared finding the genius of the place a requirement for good garden design, an eighteenth century idea that's still respected today, whether or not it's actually practised.

The term can be taken to mean the "essence" or "unique quality" of a given area. Every site is different, from its physical makeup to its soil biology to its role in the water and weather cycles flowing through it. Finding its essence is important if you hope to understand and enter into a deeper relationship with it.

The trouble with finding the "spirit of a place" is that it can take time. We live in a hyper era where we're apt to believe we can visit somewhere, take a good look around and instantly know the place. Perhaps we can, in some measure, but maybe not in ways that matter.

To genuinely know a place is to live with it and see how it changes every day, through the seasons, and to watch what plants and animals it supports over the years, which are never the same twice. In earlier times when we were less mobile this tie to the land would be a generational legacy. We would know a place not only through our own experience but through the lessons of our parents and elders as well.

Today we may not have that rich a library of wisdom to call on. If that's the case, we have to work that much harder.

Saving the Earth is an outdoor job. If you rarely go outside, or when you do, if you pay little attention, how can you know where you really stand?

There are Japanese people born and raised in big cities who say they've never seen a star. Shocking as this would sound to some, many North Americans would be hard-pressed to draw an accurate arc of the sun across the winter sky, or map where the water coming out of their kitchen taps fell to the Earth.

Living in a city means it can take more effort to understand the nature we're trying to save. It doesn't happen naturally the way it would have when most of us were farmers. It doesn't happen much at all in school, although science class and the peas grown in paper cups probably help.

You could get a decent guidebook or find some nifty apps that would likely be useful. But the best route is to do it yourself, when you're outside, by slowing down long enough to observe.

Joachim Radkau writes in the epilogue to *Nature and Power: A Global History of the Environment*:

> Donald Worster was right when he said that it was important "to get out of doors altogether, and to ramble Into fields, woods, and the open air. It is time we bought a good set of walking shoes, and we cannot avoid getting some mud on them." Through hiking, biking and swimming, we refresh our emotional relationship to nature, become healthier, and even make surprising

discoveries about environmental history. Environmental historians must never forget that much in the human relationship to the environment is not articulated, that one discovers it better on hikes than in books.

So go outside. Find a place that means something to you. Don't worry about looking for "wilderness" or going to the "environment" or choosing somewhere that has "nature." As we've seen, they're everywhere.

Your special place could be anywhere under the sky: a meadow buzzing with insects or a park bench covered with snow or a noisy city intersection. It just has to be a piece of the Earth, and it has to be important enough that you would select it. Then you're ready to groundtruth it.

Plant your feet on the ground and look. Listen. Breathe. *Feel.* Your connection to the living planet is beneath your feet and in the air moving around you. What else there is alive?

How did this land get to its present state? Is it healthy? Beautiful? Who was here before? Did the land provide for them? Who or what does it feed now?

And how do you fit in? Are you this land's owner, servant, partner, just a visitor passing through, or maybe all of the above in various combinations at different times?

If the land you're on is not as healthy as it could be, why not? Or if it is, does anything threaten it from staying that way? In either case, is it worth saving?

If so, how far would you go? If not for you, is it worth saving for your children or grandchildren or any concept of future generations you can summon?

You could do this in gratitude for all those who tended the land to get it to the state you see it today, or you could pay it forward to those in the future. You might do it because your conscience commands you now that it has considered this idea: one day, when children are studying our era on the brink, one of them might ask you: "During that crazy time when everyone knew the Earth was burning, what did *you* do?"

Your site should be a place where you want to spend time. It doesn't have to be spectacular. It doesn't even have to be comfortable. You're interested in it as a piece of nature that needs you as much as you need it, so even a degraded site would be valid. You want somewhere you can spend time in because that's what it takes to slow down long enough to find the rhythm of the land.

One suggestion for those unable to find a worthy site is to start in a local community garden. There the politics of building a better world can be found right at your feet and worked through with shovels and meetings. You may learn how to create your own alternative to the capitalist notion of what is good and right and desirable in this life as you tend the land together to produce a bounty of fresh, organic food.

For many, their special place will be right in their own yard or garden. This can be a good way to start and to get your hands into the soil. Once you do, taking into account the ecology of the space and everything it's connected to, you'll realize how it's an ecosystem and connected to the world beyond.

Even if all you have is a balcony, you can help it find its role in support of a greener planet by growing a few things in containers. This may not provide the same immersive experience as a hike through a deep forest, but it will heighten your interest in the elements. You're more apt to monitor the sun to gauge growing opportunities for your tomatoes and look for coming weather patterns for signs of rain or heat or cold that might affect your blooms. If you've planted things for butterflies or birds, wonderful; you're adding to biodiversity. If you've planted food for yourself, it's still wonderful. Either way you'll become more intimately involved with the bounty of your bioregion, and the critters will benefit too.

If you've looked and thought and still haven't found a place, go for a walk. A stroll makes an excellent pace for observation. When you walk, you experience the world at the same speed as our earlier ancestors.

Leave the cell phone and the MP3 player at home. This walk doesn't have to be an escape. Instead make it a journey to something, perhaps greater understanding and appreciation. For that you want to be aware.

Places in our own cities may seem dull in comparison to some national park wilderness areas, and less inspiring, but they are just as important. In a strategic sense they may even be more useful.

A living example of nature in a city will be

experienced by multitudes every day. Every person who does so may become a potential partner of the Earth, someone who could decide to become *engagé* as well. In an age of images, the opportunity to teach a lesson with land and plants is invaluable.

Another reason to get involved in your own city is that a better world begins as soon as you get off the couch. There's no quicker antidote for urban dread than to start working on a solution. People filling sand bags in the face of an oncoming flood do not moan about the future. They get exhilarated by the challenge and discover bonds with neighbours they may never have known were there.

Getting involved also helps us locate ourselves. Over time, if that time is spent respectfully in conversation with a particular piece of land, we may even feel grounded.

With enough seasons of experience, watching and being with the land in a variety of weather, we may come to consider ourselves native to a place – although we have to tread carefully when using that term. Substitute "local" if it helps avoid confusion.

In any case it wouldn't do to ignore the recent history of the land of the places we now set out to save. You cannot understand a site without knowledge of the people it may have supported through generations. Anything you can discover about the technology of living on that land from the cultures which did so would be valuable.

By "native" or "local" we mean to recognize a person who has spent enough time being with the land to feel at home there. At that level of involvement we begin to understand ourselves as being integral to the part, which means we can also be integral to the whole.

We might then know we have a role to play in defending that land because of its importance not just to us but to the wider network of life. We cast our fate together with our place, and marry its prospects to all the other connected places.

Can this really happen in a crowded city? Rather than think of the reasons why not, consider instead that it must.

Cities in the twenty-first century are who we are. If we don't get urban areas right, we don't get the rest of the planet right either.

It's an enormous task but that needn't

discourage us. Nor should we be daunted by the legacy of past civilizations that have failed, as suggested in the brief list that began this chapter.

We're in new territory now, building cities with a new understanding. Even in the living memory of our elders it was once believed that flying was restricted to birds, so who knows what we'll think 100 years from now?

In any event, our connection to nature is something that must be continually renewed, so it's not as if we figure this out once and we're done. One we get engaged, we stay that way.

There is a climate imperative here, and now is obviously the best time to start, but you needn't feel rushed to settle on a place to groundtruth. Engaged Ecology is a process that begins as soon as you develop the notion to do it, so you may already be making progress.

The discovery of your particular site can happen in time. Land has its own rhythm. It moves slower than we do. We can't match it, but we can sit and pay attention and on some level come to know it.

Feel free to do this in a number of places until you find a site that fits. There are countless opportunities through places that begin right outside your door. You just have to start. The most important step is the first one, and it's been taken by everyone who has ever become *engagé*.

We Have the Right to Clean Air, Pure Water, Healthy Soil

Who decided it was acceptable to live in a world where 12,000 people die every year from poisoned air?

Who voted for an environment where the first mother's milk our newborns swallow includes pesticides and paint thinner and flame retardant?

Who agreed to a global economy where a forest the size of 36 football fields gets cut down every minute?

If any of these facts seem upsetting, get upset. We've been too quiet too long. No one asks our permission before committing crimes against the world, but if we just let them do it, we're part of the problem. That has to end. When we see a wrong, we need to speak up to oppose it. We must confront those responsible.

There's no shortage of good causes to support

and bad people to fight in the campaign for a greener Earth. Once you choose a place and discover the range of its connections, it won't take long to find groups to help you protect it from the people who would wreck anything to fatten a bottom line.

Local politics – the level of decision-making that may most directly affect your site – is a first step. It's where the changes we determine can happen the soonest in ways we get to see.

But we mustn't lose sight of the causes, where the real problems lie. Get rid of some bad business people and rotten politicians and watch what happens: new ones take their place and are just as horrible. The problem goes deeper than a few greedy individuals or evil corporations. It's the system that keeps producing them.

The capitalist model of success based on perpetual growth is no longer appropriate, if it ever was. Our understanding of ecology tells us why it couldn't have lasted. We can't just trash a place and move on, when the places are all connected.

Too bad it took the fouling of some beautiful areas of the planet before the lesson became clear. Also too bad that although the results are obvious, the binge is still going on. We know it's madness but we don't see an alternative, or else we're afraid to think one all the way through.

So invasive is the reach of the current system, it has imprinted itself like a brand onto our minds. We're afraid to whisper in public the prospect of anything that might challenge it. Suggest a view of capitalism that treats it as something less than a divine inspiration and you're called a terrorist or, worse, a socialist. Now you may as well admit you snatch babies in your spare time.

We should stop being afraid of the bullies who guard a system that's failing the Earth. We need to stand up to them. We have to tell them the truth: that the status quo equals death and a better way is our only hope of survival.

Precisely what that better way will be is still to be determined – but not by the same wealthy manipulators who got us into this mess.

The struggle for a healthy environment has so many fronts that you could pick your particular battle and be happily engaged in it for a lifetime. Your take on our campaign doesn't have to be defined as a political choice between capitalism and something else.

Many people are trying to discover the best way to live together on a healthy planet. For some it means seeing the conflict with a narrower focus. Opposing Monsanto's quest to own the future of agriculture through the control of seeds, for example, or stopping the mass experiment private corporations are carrying out on the public with their genetically modified food.

Don't let the glut of possibilities be stifling. Pick a scale and cause that resonates for you. The most important thing is to join in. Politics is a numbers game. When we have enough of us standing together on the same side to challenge the system, we'll win.

How far should we go?

We should be as radical as our times. Radical, from the Latin *radix* for "root," means looking beyond the symptoms to deal with the cause of a problem.

This idea forms the basis for action on which *The Earth Manifesto* turns. It allows us to ask whether it would be enough to see our problems as solvable through whack-a-mole environmental clean-ups and more sustainable growth.

Radical change can be scary. In the politics

we're more used to, we try for improvements by adding up small victories shaped out of compromise, often through elections.

We win some and lose more. We like to believe we're gradually getting better this way, but the facts don't lie. Inequality has mushroomed in the past 30 years. Almost everyone but the wealthy is working harder to get less on a deteriorating planet. More species are dying and the atmosphere is still heating up.

It's now clear the changes we need are bigger and bolder than anything we've tried so far. And they have to come sooner rather than later.

We need to transform society. It has to begin with individual awareness. That can happen if we reflect on our rightful role in nature through the sites we choose for groundtruthing. But it doesn't end there.

The next step involves understanding how these places grow or die according to the political ecosystem in which they're located. No place is an island and no site exists free of the power structure that rules the land. A perfect oasis is not an escape if its foundation is corrupt. Once we've decided to protect our special places, we have to examine where the threats are coming from and then deal with them at the root level.

In trying this, we open ourselves up. When we give up the facade of being unaffected, which is the urban default mode for too many of us, we reveal our own vulnerability.

We have to accept the fact that the solutions are not easy. The issues are rarely as simple as good versus evil, and even when they are, we must recognize we have some of both within us.

Until we figure out how to live in harmony with each other and the environment, we should acknowledge that our own starting positions are compromised and that we don't have all the answers we need to make a clear run to victory.

But that's no reason not to start. It's a process we need to engage in. Along the way we'll discover creative ways to challenge the destructive forces threatening our future.

Seeing the struggle in these epic terms is admitting we take it as a big deal, and that means big risks, with victory not at all assured. There is always the prospect we will lose. It takes a lot of battles to add up to a victory, and in any one of them any one of us could lose everything.

The shrinking rainforest home of the indigenous Penan hunter-gatherers in Sarawak attracted a Swiss activist named Bruno Manser to Malaysia in 1984. He chose a remote place to make his stand – not the recommended approach and one fraught with all kinds of cultural complications. But if it was to be a conversation with nature, this was a site that screamed. You would need to be a timber investor or government accomplice to be deaf to the pleas as the last pure rivers on that island turned yellow. Manser lived for six years with the Penan, learning the language and becoming an international spokesperson for their survival. After he was declared an "enemy of the state" in 2000, the Malaysian army was sent into the jungle to track him down. He has never been seen since and was legally declared dead in 2005.

Almir Nogueira de Amorim and João Luiz Telles Penetra were Brazilian fishermen in Rio de Janeiro who opposed a plan by Petrobras to construct a gas pipeline that would have destroyed the fishery. The group they led called itself the Association of Sea Men. Their bodies were found on the last day of the Rio+20 Earth Summit in 2012. They had been bound at the hands and feet.

Almir was tied to a boat and João washed up on the shore of Guanabara Bay.

Nigerian writer Ken Saro-Wiwa led his Ogoni people in a non-violent campaign to save their homeland, Ogoniland, from environmental destruction by the oil giant Shell. Rich foreign corporations do not expect opposition in the poor countries where they do business, and the Nigerian government was pressured to stop the protests. Saro-Wiwa was arrested, tried and convicted by the military government in 1995. In a statement before he was hanged with eight other leaders, he said of Shell that "its day will surely come. The crime of the company's dirty wars against the Ogoni people will be punished." Some consumers today still refuse to gas up at a Shell station. Sued in a US court by Saro-Wiwa's son for participating in atrocities including torture, illegal detention, forced exile, and murder, Shell settled in 2009. In an important precedent on corporate responsibility, Shell, although not admitting guilt, paid the victim's families $15.5-million.

More than 700 people have been killed in the past decade for trying to protect the Earth. This figure comes from a report by the non-profit group Global Witness. That's more than a martyr a week, but the actual figure is higher, since these are only the reported murders reaching Global Witness researchers. They added that the violence is likely to increase as tensions rise between corporations and people over dwindling resources. The murder rate of activists in 2011 was said to be twice that of 2009.

If any of these crimes seem maddening, get mad. We need more angry people. Not to rage, because we have to be smarter than that, and we have to be the ones in control. And not to lose focus by attacking the front men, who may be no more than mercenaries for their corporate masters. Again, our problem is not a few bad apples but the system that props them up.

To take that on, we need mass support, people with the courage to stand tall even though the consequences could be fatal. The saddest part of the martyrs' stories is not the tragedy still weighing on their families and communities, but that they may have died in vain.

"We Have the Right to Clean Air, Pure Water, Healthy Soil." These rights should be written into every declaration of human rights everywhere on Earth.

They're suggested here as human rights because humans will have to press for justice in human-run legislatures and courts. It's a strategy, but it may not be the best one. If people are just one part of nature, and not necessarily the centre, why must all rights filter through them? Why not get to the heart of the matter and insist the Earth itself has rights? That way we could stop any polluting corporation on behalf of the environment. Either of these approaches should be valid if the results are the same: protection by law of our common Earth.

Ideas like this drive the oligarch class mad. Watch how their media attack dogs come out snarling. Anyone proposing these rights is ridiculed for woolly-headed dreaming. The very notion is ridiculed as preposterous, unthinkable, crazy, disruptive. Which is how rights are always denied, until the stubborn people who won't stop fighting for them eventually win and suddenly these unfathomable ideas are as normal as sunshine.

This is how rights are made real, through a

long struggle just to get to the obvious. So we claim these rights as if they already exist, because they do; they just haven't been recognized.

That is, they haven't been in North America. The Constitution of Ecuador does recognize the right of nature to exist, to have its ecosystems restored and its life cycles preserved. Nature figures prominently in the government's principle of Buen Vivir, or Good Living, an alternative approach to development based more on community than on profit. The concept arose out of traditional wisdom contributed by indigenous activist groups in Ecuador, and made it all the way to the national law of the land. In a public referendum in 2008, the new constitution was approved in a landslide.

UBC professor David Boyd says some form of rights for the environment appears in the laws of more than 100 countries. A blurb for his book *The Environmental Rights Revolution* says these nations "have stronger environmental laws, enhanced enforcement, greater government accountability and better access to justice, information and public participation in decision making" than those without. The result, he found, is countries have smaller ecological footprints and can deal more quickly with pollution problems.

Claiming these rights is a way to get the legal tools needed to defend our home, but they don't come into effect only once they're adopted. As offered here they're meant to be a starting point for discussion, not the complete version.

Whether the best strategy is through human or Earth-based rights, the effects of environmental degradation are unavoidably felt by people, and usually the poorest people, the ones who can't afford to mitigate or move away from pollution.

Like women's rights and civil rights, what may seem at first to be sector-based campaigns are actually universal because no society can be healthy with such glaring flaws in its structure. The rights claimed here are bound to the physical Earth, in ways that should make the tragedy of their absence painfully clear.

We Have the Right to Clean Air. Who would deny us the necessity to breathe? Those who suffer most from the lack of clean air, typically society's weakest members such as infants, the elderly and the ill, should not have to pay with their lives for the political shortcomings of their leaders. Anyone responsible for choking the airways should be held to account, together with any officials who let it happen. The day a prominent corporate executive or political leader appears in a criminal court to answer for this crime will be the beginning of our shift to less pollution and clearer skies.

We Have the Right to Pure Water. More children die every year from water-borne illness than from any other cause. The global well has been poisoned. No family should have to watch their baby suffer because the local system cannot provide pure water. The Earth didn't do this to itself. Someone released the pollutants and someone failed to provide even a rudimentary system of drinking water that can sustain life. The Earth has a miraculous natural hydrological system that continually replenishes itself, but in the places where people have ruined it, it must be repaired and those responsible for the ruin must be brought to justice.

We Have the Right to Healthy Soil. The fact that pesticides are now in our own bloodstreams is unacceptable, as is the massive loss of topsoil, that thin strip of the Earth on which our food supply depends. It will be too late to try to get it back once it's gone. We have to reverse this trend by changing the system that's stealing the living layer of soil off our own land.

We claim these rights on behalf of a healthy planet. Wherever they're denied, that government loses legitimacy. It can either improve or let someone else try.

We have a duty to oppose any entity, public or private, which would destroy our home. We join our fellow citizens of the Earth, on behalf of all organisms in the great web of biodiversity, to stand for life.

Engaged Ecology Creates a Community

Never doubt that a small group of thoughtful, committed citizens can seriously fuck up the world. Indeed, it is the only thing that ever has.

If a tiny, rich class of elites can have so much effect, imagine what the rest of us can do, working together, with less money, to be sure, but far greater numbers and a lot more heart.

The world we're designing depends on groups of thoughtful, committed citizens who care about their communities and will resist anything that would destroy them. When enough of these groups focus their power in the same direction, the Earth we love will be saved.

It all comes back to place and motivation. Beyond lofty ideas and empty slogans, Engaged Ecology is a way for people in real locations to explore what a place is truly worth. Not in its real estate value, but in its worth to the community through the web of life that supports us.

If a place is deemed valuable, and recognized as a part of nature, and offers us a chance to explore our own relationship with the wilderness, it can inspire a commitment that binds people to resonate through generations.

Gary Snyder explains in *The Real Works: Interviews and Talks 1964–1979*:

> To say "we must dig in" or "here we must draw our line" is a far more universal application than growing your own food or living in the country. One of the key problems in American society now, it seems to me, is people's lack of commitment to any given place – which, again, is totally unnatural and outside of history. Neighborhoods are allowed to deteriorate, landscapes are allowed to be strip-mined, because there is nobody who will live there and take responsibility; they'll just move on.

This commitment may start with one person but it doesn't stay there. That person typically shares the gift of the place with others who also commit to it, or else shares the effort involved in saving it with other people defending other places. Every alliance we make multiplies the possibilities of success.

Joining others who understand your passion is a critical step toward developing the collective energy that can make a difference. As soon as you stand together, you've moved from thinking to doing and have cleared that first hurdle which stops most people.

It's also where your vision can broaden, almost without limits. We learn there's more to our campaign than a single pond or city park or housing development or even urban master plan. When we understand how our cause is connected to countless others, we gain an insight that will be useful when we're confronted with challenges that would be too huge to imagine tackling alone. Engaged Ecology Creates a Community.

Seeing our goals as a group effort brings us back to the idea with which this book began: interdependence. One person identifying with a place makes it more likely that others will identify with theirs. Visible acts of dedication become mutually supporting as the people behind them then collaborate.

Curiously, it's through nurturing a bond to the land that we can strengthen our ties to people. If they turn out to be people we like or respect, so much the better. Some of them may even end up being seen as our heroes, and vice versa.

Once past the phony celebrity worship of supermarket magazines and TV chatter, who would you really believe to be worth emulating? You may find it's the people in your own community who give themselves to it: the dedicated teacher, the tireless soccer coach, the volunteer reader for the blind.

Environmental heroes work on the same level, whether or not they realize how their gift of time and energy doesn't stop but gets passed on. When you link your fate together with people who share a passion for the Earth, you've already created a community that can get things done.

"Many hands make light work," the saying goes, but saving the Earth is never going to be easy. Working with others, even enthusiastic volunteers, is still work.

Social interactions take more energy than we

tend to realize. You don't need to feel guilty if you feel tired and would prefer a comfortable sofa at home over a plastic seat in a meeting room where someone is bound to natter on too long. It's also okay to be wary of the prospect of joining a group to talk and talk about how a difficult job should be done. Who among us isn't inwardly happy to hear an upcoming meeting has been cancelled? Burnout is an occupational hazard that threatens anyone drawn to political activism.

Yet people still show up, put in their time and pour incredible energy into causes that may never be realized. Why?

Everyone comes to a movement with their own motivations beyond the obvious shared goal. Something rarely considered is how community work benefits those involved. Volunteers will sometimes say they do it because they get more than they give. This may sound like mush but you can prove it anytime you like simply by signing on to something important.

Hanging out with passionate people is stimulating. You get to hear stories that may be inspiring, gather local news, develop new skills, share laughs, and eventually, if things go well, get something done.

Working together can also serve as an anti-dote to our epidemic of urban alienation. If the loneliness is caused by being detached from the living world around you, we've seen already how reconnecting with nature can help. Doing it in a way that also connects you to your own species is a double dose.

Once you get into group work, it just feels right. It takes us back to our ancestral beginnings as members of a clan surviving together in a dangerous world.

Working with others has the added possibil-ity, which should be a requirement, of being fun.

The social perks are mentioned here as a re-minder of things you probably already knew and to help motivate anyone still on the fence. But even without these things, we would still have to take up the fight, and join others who care, because ... what else are we going to do?

We've already discarded apathy as a strategy and we've seen how pessimism is self-defeating. Neither temptation can last once we get together with others.

Joe Strummer put it this way:

I'd like to say that people can change
anything they want to; and that means
everything in the world. Show me any
country and there'll be people in it. And it's
the people that make the country. People
have got to stop pretending they're not on
the world. People are running about following their little tracks. I am one of them. But
we've all got to just stop following our own
little mouse trail. People can do anything;
this is something that I'm beginning to
learn. People are out there doing bad things
to each other; it's because they've been
dehumanized. It's time to take that humanity
back into the centre of the ring and follow
that for a time. Greed … it ain't going
anywhere! They should have that on a big
billboard across Times Square. Think on
that. Without people you're nothing … that's
my spiel.

The future of the Earth is too important to
leave to individuals who either don't care or

think they can make the difference on their own. We know it will take a community, working with other communities, to achieve meaningful change. Fortunately, that's precisely what we become when we practise Engaged Ecology: a community.

How and what to join must be determined according to your own situation. If it helps, start small. Size does matter in group work, and small ones are easier to start or join. They have the advantage over a mass movement in keeping the shared experiences to an approachable, human scale. History has had enough examples of the individual being submerged under the will of a demagogue and his adoring crowds.

Participating through small groups lets us know what our contribution means through immediate feedback. The results are easy to interpret. The boycott call either goes out or it doesn't; the letter to the editor either gets written or is forgotten.

A small group with plans and action items also lets us see how we're now a part of the solution and thus no longer powerless.

Small groups may be less intimidating for those reluctant to join a political campaign for fear they won't get along with others. The extreme example of this category would be the survivalists, those unfortunate few who sense looming disruptions to our networks of energy, transportation, food and more and then come up with their own solution that's entirely out of whack.

Hunkering down behind steel barriers with guns and tinned food is no way to live, especially not when it goes against our own history of responding to collective threats with co-operation. The apocalypse some of these people expect is in their own minds already, as they mistakenly see in their fellow human beings not a community to be built together but enemies in the making.

All the more reason to hone our skills now at coming together to work on common challenges. The better we know our neighbours and how they perform on shared tasks in good times, the better we'll be able to help each other get through the troubles.

Our goal is a cooler planet where life thrives. The campaign to keep the planet healthy will never be over.

It may be one of those quests that's more about the journey than the goal. The important part now is how we get moving in the right direction. Joachim Radkau says in *Nature and Power* that some environmentalists, seeing the failure of our political systems to handle climate change, secretly dream of an ecological dictatorship, but "that would only worsen the problems of the connection between nature protection and power ... the lesson of history is unambiguous: effective environmental protection requires a spirited civil society, the courage of one's convictions, citizen initiatives and a critical public."

This is how we create the culture. Not the bland culture of capitalist exploitation that treats nature as a commodity and people as a human resource, but our own definition of the world we want in which nature is here and wilderness is within and our cities are alive because they're full of connected people.

Political and environmental groups abound. If you can't find one that fits your vision, start it.

A town or small city can provide an ideal population from which to recruit members to share the work of saving the sites we know are important. In a big city these self-defining community groups may be more difficult to realize, but perhaps not if you define them by street or neighbourhood or district.

By coming back to the land, natural subcultures can develop organically even in a megacity. You may find a polluted stream an appropriate organizing tool. Maybe you're interested in greening the stark environment of the local industrial park. On a bigger scale, a watershed can serve as a natural way to define a population with shared interests. So too can a bioregion.

No single approach can be recommended to work everywhere, since each place will have its own population and characteristics and culture. The best strategies will always go back to taking their lessons from the land.

Once we've decided to form or join a group, what next?

Start by defining or clarifying your purpose. Many do this with a mission statement, a proclamation stating the reason for the group. Heifer International's mission is "to work with communities to end hunger and poverty and care for the Earth." The Environmental Justice Foundation "believes environmental security is a human right."

When it comes to grand statements of intent, the fewer words and the less jargon the better. Rather than "respect the environment" or "foster sustainable behaviour," narrow the focus down into what you're going to do.

The point of a mission statement is to set your group on a steady course. It will also provide something you can consult later when inevitable questions arise over whether you're doing the right thing with one tactic or another. Note that a mission statement isn't carved in stone. It's acceptable, and even desirable, to revisit and revise your mission statement as your group and its campaign develops.

Your cause may be environmental, which is logical given the sites we're called to preserve. But no place's environment exists in isolation from the politics and economics around it.

For too long we've let ourselves be divided by lines that shouldn't be there separating the ecology folks from the union supporters from the anti-poverty activists. The principles, culture, styles, lingo and more have been allowed to develop in separate camps, making it harder for us to see how our issues are actually shared and our adversaries the same.

This doesn't mean you have to take it upon yourself to bridge these gaps, just that it may be worth keeping in mind that we're unlikely to build a unifying movement until we all learn to get along. A healthy green world will not be built on the backs of exploited workers, and no political group can successfully change society without solving the environmental crisis that threatens it.

Every group will have its own goals and strategies to get there. With so much to be done and only so much time and energy to do it, choices have to be made.

Is it worth taking part in elections? Candidates make excellent listeners, at least until election day. Ask directly about their understanding of your environmental issue and what they propose to do about it. Non-answers should be met with non-votes, and explanations why.

In other cases, mobilization for the parliament of the streets may be more effective. History has countless examples where elections did little but the mighty were finally brought down when confronted by people in mass numbers.

We said earlier how politics moves by numbers. So does economics. Direct action that targets the source of a problem at its financial base has a rich history, although oddly it seems to be used less frequently in recent years.

Is a company in your area polluting a waterway? Organize a boycott if you're convinced you can get the support it will take to succeed. If that particular company doesn't have a product or service to refuse, check its corporate ties. The trend to consolidation has created some huge targets in the multinational corporations that now control surprising percentages of the market.

The fact that we may not even recognize the names of some of the most dominant corporations responsible for our food, clothing and daily necessities speaks to how far removed we've let ourselves become. But it's not hard to follow the money trail with a little research. Start with the subsidiaries and move up the food chain to the head corporation; then strike wherever works best. No boardroom is comfortable with the potential for bad publicity.

The environmental movement today is in a miserable state. Given the glaring problems now even affecting the weather, it's hard to understand why the whole world isn't pressing for solutions.

In the first Earth Summit in Rio de Janeiro in 1992, environmentalists from around the planet got together to puzzle over a map of the future that would let us live in it. For better or worse, the key concept for the past 20 years guiding our approach to the limits of the natural world has been "sustainable development."

How that notion made it to the top of the flagpole is too long a story to go into here. It has its logic, but really? Sustain *this*? Also, a milder form of *development*? That's the best we've got? A concept so inoffensive a million corporations now spout it in every website and year-end report?

When the world got together in 2012 for Rio+20, it seemed clear the bloom was off the rose. Thousands of good people showed up and the debates went on, but who even listened? What changed? In what place did the bonfire of fossil fuels diminish or the growing inequalities slow down?

The future can seem a bleak place to be heading

into. The facts suggest our hands may be bloody already in causing a mass extinction of species to rival the dinosaur die-off. We may have set in motion an unstoppable process of environmental destruction.

In any field we can imagine – politics, economics, spirituality and more – we can see cracks in the structure, and yet our thoughts are distracted by dodges and trifles. Arguments erupt not over how our kids can survive but whether wind farms are useful or ugly. What hope do we have?

In *The Earth Only Endures* Jules Pretty asks:

> Will modern globalized society become number 41 on the list of departed civilizations? Or might there come another phase in human history, where we recognize the critical importance of the environment in making us who we are, and appreciate that harm to this world harms us too?

Pretty holds out the prospect of a further phase of human history centred on survival of the greenest, which he calls "ecolution." For this to happen, he says, "We are going to need, at the very least, a better story."

Take heart. One thing we're good at is stories. They help give us hope, which is something we can build on. We didn't make it this far in evolution by being hand-wringers and worriers.

Know that a shift is happening already. Plenty of people are dedicated to a better, greener world. You do not have to come up with a solution on your own. And you will not be left to fend for yourself. You already have allies by the millions who agree that things are bad, and this means it's time to roll up our sleeves.

Good news stories can be found everywhere you look – although you do have to look, since they aren't the kind of thing favoured by TV news producers or headline writers. (Side note to keep in mind: TV is a drug.)

Transition Towns are already building local networks to support the community if an environmental calamity or oil shortage disrupts the global economy. People in these areas are already developing the resilience to survive stresses – which is a definition of health in a human body.

The Slow Food movement is encouraging

alternatives to the industrial farming system. Urban farmers are redesigning cities plot by plot to make them better food producers. By selling produce directly to people (not "consumers"; *people*) they're creating alternatives to a global market economy in which Walmart has become the world's biggest grocery store.

We're evolving rapidly into our future as an urban species with a new relationship to cities. Critical to this reboot will be how we connect to nature.

The city of the future must be built by and for communities of people who have come together to share their commitment to preserve the natural Earth.

Who knows just what shape these cities will take? Probably not the science fiction fare of gleaming chrome towers and happy people in white jumpsuits flying with personal jetpacks. Expect surprises.

But our cities will be alive and they will look like it. So there will be plenty of green growth, and also decay, messy areas, crowded places, quiet spots, wilderness throughout and whatever else that goes into making up a healthy environment.

The future will be determined by those willing to put in the work today. Anyone who believes a better world is possible is lucky to live in such a dynamic time. The opportunities to lead a meaningful life are everywhere.

Just as we're connected through interdependence, we share the potential to engage with nature in a collective practice that will change history. We're all in this together.

Bookshelf

Boyd, David Richard. *The Environmental Rights Revolution: A Global Study of Constitutions, Human Rights, and the Environment*. Vancouver: UBC Press, 2012.

Jensen, Derek. *How Shall I Live My Life? On Liberating The Earth from Civilization*. Oakland: PM Press, 2008.

Pollan, Michael. *Second Nature: A Gardener's Education*. New York: Atlantic Monthly Press, 1991.

Pretty, Jules. *The Earth Only Endures: On Reconnecting With Nature and Our Place in It*. London: Earthscan, 2007.

Radkau, Joachim. *Nature and Power: A Global History of the Environment*. New York: Cambridge University Press, 2008.

Ricard, Matthieu, and Trinh Xuan Thuan. *The Quantum and the Lotus*. New York: Crown Publishers, 2001.

Schaefer, Valentin, Hillary Rudd and Jamie Vala. *Urban Biodiversity: Exploring Natural Habitat and Its Value in Cities*. Concord: Captus Press, 2004.

Shepard, Paul, and Florence R. Shepard. *Coming Home to the Pleistocene*. Washington, DC: Island Press, 1998.

Snyder, Gary. *The Practice of the Wild*. San Francisco: North Point Press, 1990.

Snyder, Gary, and William Scott McLean. *The Real Work: Interviews & Talks, 1964–1979*. New York: New Directions, 1980.

Suzuki, David, with Amanda McConnell and Adrienne Mason. *The Sacred Balance: Rediscovering Our Place In Nature*. Vancouver: Greystone Books, 2007.

Other Titles in this Series

Saving Lake
Winnipeg

Robert William
Sandford

David Tracey

ISBN 978-1-927330-86-9

The
Homeward
Wolf

Kevin Van Tighem

ISBN 978-1-927330-83-8

On Fracking

C. Alexia Lane

ISBN 978-1-927330-80-7

Little Black Lies

Corporate and
Political Spin
in the Global War
for Oil

Jeff Gailus

ISBN 978-1-926855-68-4

Digging the City

An Urban
Agriculture
Manifesto

Rhona McAdam

ISBN 978-1-927330-21-0

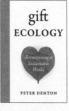

Gift Ecology

Reimagining a
Sustainable World

Peter Denton

ISBN 978-1-927330-40-1

The Insatiable Bark Beetle

Dr. Reese Halter

ISBN 978-1-926855-67-7

The Incomparable Honeybee

and the Economics
of Pollination
Revised & Updated

Dr. Reese Halter

ISBN 978-1-926855-65-3

The Beaver Manifesto

Glynnis Hood

ISBN 978-1-926855-58-5

The Grizzly Manifesto

In Defence of the Great Bear

Jeff Gailus

ISBN 978-1-897522-83-7

Becoming Water

Glaciers in a Warming World

Mike Demuth

ISBN 978-1-926855-72-1

Ethical Water

Learning To Value What Matters Most

Robert William Sandford & Merrell-Ann S. Phare

ISBN 978-1-926855-70-7

Denying the Source

The Crisis of First Nations Water Rights

Merrell-Ann S. Phare

ISBN 978-1-897522-61-5

The Weekender Effect

Hyperdevelopment in Mountain Towns

Robert William Sandford

ISBN 978-1-897522-10-3

RMB saved the following resources by printing the pages of this book on chlorine-free paper made with 100% post-consumer waste:

Trees · 6, fully grown
Water · 2,850 gallons
Energy · 2 million BTUs
Solid Waste · 191 pounds
Greenhouse Gases · 526 pounds

CALCULATIONS BASED ON RESEARCH BY ENVIRONMENTAL DEFENSE AND THE PAPER TASK FORCE. MANUFACTURED AT FRIESENS CORPORATION.